WHAT IS MY DESTINY?

WHAT IS MY DESTINY?

Text by Sally Brockway

An Hachette UK Company
www.hachette.co.uk

Summersdale Publishers Ltd
Part of Octopus Publishing Group Limited
Carmelite House
50 Victoria Embankment
LONDON
EC4Y 0DZ
UK

www.summersdale.com

Printed and bound in China

ISBN: 978-1-80007-420-0

Substantial discounts on bulk quantities of Summersdale books are available to corporations, professional associations and other organizations. For details contact general enquiries: telephone: +44 (0) 1243 771107 or email: enquiries@summersdale.com.

WHAT IS MY DESTINY?

A Guided Journal to Help You
Unlock the Secrets of Your Future

ASTRID CARVEL

summersdale

To ....

From ....

INTRODUCTION

Would you like to know what's in store for you tomorrow, next week or even years down the line? If the answer to this question is "yes", you are not alone. History tells us that people have always been interested in predicting the future. In ancient times, those who could foretell events were highly regarded and known as prophets, and, later on, civilizations turned to the stars or numbers to make predictions.

Many of the different forms of fortune telling that have been used for centuries are still practised today, and you don't have to be psychic, religious or trained to use them. With the help of this journal, you can explore the most popular methods and use them as a guide to help you navigate life.

The purpose of these practices is not to predict the future with 100 per cent accuracy. The results will be open to your own interpretation, and if you enter into each method with an open mind and a relaxed attitude, you'll gain something from every reading. You'll get to know yourself better, have a clearer idea of what you want from life and, as you continue to practise, you'll find yourself tapping into some awesome magic.

Your destiny awaits – are you ready to discover what's in store?

PALMISTRY

Palmistry is a way of determining personality traits and future life events by looking at the lines on the palm of the hand. The left hand shows character traits, while the right predicts the future (this is for right-handed people, the reverse for left-handed ones).

There are four main lines on the palm:

Life line – A common mistake is to assume that this line represents how long you are going to live. It actually predicts major life events, health issues and well-being. The deeper it is, the more your life will be jam-packed with experiences. A short line indicates an independent spirit and strong will.

Heart line – This signifies your emotional state and relationships with others. If it begins below the index finger, you are content in your relationship, if it begins below the middle finger, you feel restless and could be thinking about finding someone new. Breaks in the line represent your lovers.

Head line – This represents wisdom, intellect and the strength of your intuitive abilities. It is also a mark of the lessons you are destined to learn in this lifetime. If it is deep, then your fate is complex. If there are breaks in the head line, they could point to a breakthrough moment or a struggle. If your head line starts on the life line and moves out from there, it means you have a strong mind. A fork represents writing ability.

Fate line – Running up the palm toward your middle finger, the fate line can span the length of the palm or be as short as an inch. A few people don't have one, but this just means they are free spirits. If you have a short fate line, you are someone with a butterfly mind who likes to flit from one thing to the next. A long, deep fate line shows that you are determined and likely to succeed in life.

Take a look at the picture of the palm below, which shows a faint outline of where the four major lines are situated. Draw yours onto the diagram and write down what you notice. Is one line particularly deep? Do any of them branch off?

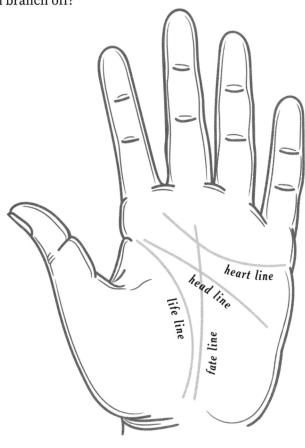

....

....

....

A HAND REVEALS A WORLD OF POSSIBILITIES

BIBLIOMANCY

All you need for this simple method of fortune telling is a book. Any book will do, but if you don't have one, you can also use a journal or magazine.

Relying on your instinct, pick any book or magazine, or close your eyes and run your finger along a bookshelf until you get the feeling that you've landed on the right title.

Once you have the book or magazine in your hands, close your eyes and open it. Then, open your eyes and settle upon the first word or sentence that captures your attention. This is your message. Do the words answer a question that you've been mulling over? Are they relevant to something that is happening in your life?

Write down the sentence or passage that you were shown:

....

....

....

....

....

....

Choose your words

Close your eyes and take a deep breath. When you open your eyes, look at the grid below and write down the first four words you see. These are the areas of your life that are destined to unfold favourably.

```
K  P  A  S  S  I  O  N  G  H  K  M  L  P  F
F  N  B  H  T  R  D  S  T  I  O  L  J  H  I
D  A  P  G  Y  M  X  S  J  G  Y  M  S  A  T
S  H  M  X  L  O  V  E  U  N  V  G  E  P  N
P  C  X  I  F  N  R  I  H  C  T  D  W  P  E
I  P  T  V  L  E  L  N  K  H  C  R  E  I  S
R  I  H  B  T  Y  X  K  U  S  G  E  W  N  S
I  B  E  K  Q  P  K  T  E  Q  W  H  S  E  L
T  R  A  V  E  L  X  O  K  P  L  T  A  S  N
U  Y  L  R  C  H  A  L  L  E  N  G  E  S  I
A  F  T  T  L  P  O  R  T  T  D  J  N  U  K
L  O  H  H  O  B  B  I  E  S  B  N  H  C  M
I  U  B  G  H  Y  H  T  P  O  H  C  U  F
T  A  L  E  N  T  C  A  G  J  K  L  D  B  J
Y  O  M  N  F  R  I  E  N  D  S  H  I  P  C
```

ONEIROMANCY

Oneiromancy comes from the Greek words for "dream" and "prophecy" and is the practice of using dreams to predict the future. If you dream, then you can practise oneiromancy.

When you dream, your thinking mind switches off and the power of the unconscious mind is unleashed. You are not aware of it on a day-to-day basis, but your unconscious mind is the root of all of your behavioural patterns. It often tries to communicate with you through your dreams, flagging areas of your life that need attention. Your unconscious mind is also said to be receptive to universal energies and messages.

To practise oneiromancy, sleep with a notebook by your bed so that you can jot down your dreams as soon as you wake up – otherwise you might forget them. If you get into the habit of recording and analyzing your dreams, your ability to interpret their meanings will grow over time.

Dreams and their meanings

Dreams are often loaded with symbolism. Here are some common dreams and their meanings:

Teeth falling out – Can represent a feeling of powerlessness or loss of control.

Being chased – Could mean that there is something you are avoiding in life.

Falling – Represents an area where you lack confidence and can also point to a loss of control.

Snakes – Can signify personal growth and renewal.

Drowning – Water symbolizes emotions; dreaming of drowning could indicate that you are overwhelmed by them.

Flying – Flying effortlessly suggests that you are on top of a situation; if flying is difficult, you might be struggling with something in life.

A house – Represents your inner being; finding new and hidden rooms could mean aspects of your life are set to improve.

Use this space to note down your dreams:

....

....

....

....

....

....

....

....

....

....

....

....

All the things one has forgotten scream for help in dreams.

ELIAS CANETTI

CLEROMANCY

Cleromancy is used as a way of getting a "yes" or "no" answer to a pressing question. Originally, this method of fortune telling involved picking up small objects with your eyes closed, such as sticks, bones or crystals. Nowadays, pebbles or dice are used by most.

To make your own cleromancy kit, all you need is 13 light and 13 dark pebbles of roughly the same size. Place the pebbles in a bowl or bag, close your eyes and think of the "yes" or "no" question you would most like an answer to. Shake the pebbles well and take out a handful.

If you have picked more light pebbles than dark, the answer is "yes"; more dark pebbles means "no". If you have an even number of each, then there is no answer and you'll need to try again later (allow some time to pass before you do this).

Make your own cleromancy kit

You can either collect pebbles from nature, or you can paint your own. How you decorate them is up to you – you might like to use two different colours (one light and one dark) or paint half the stones with a "Y" and the other with an "N" to indicate "yes" and "no".

Tips for painting your own pebbles

Paint the pebbles with a latex primer before applying acrylic paint. Use a fineliner to pick out details (such as the Y and N, if necessary) and, finally, coat with varnish before allowing to dry at room temperature.

SCRYING

Scrying is the art of looking at a reflective surface, such as water, and using what you see to predict the future or receive messages from the universe. This practice is sometimes referred to as hydromancy, from the Greek words for "water" and "divination". Scrying dates back to Roman times but was later banned as a forbidden art, along with other forms of fortune telling, such as black magic and palmistry, during the Renaissance period.

Why water? It is an element associated with psychic ability and intuition and is therefore the ideal vessel to carry messages. In mythology, nature spirits were said to live in fresh water and people would gaze at rivers and lakes, hoping to catch a glimpse of them.

It's a great method to try if you are new to fortune telling because all you need is water along with a curious and open mind.

TRY WATER SCRYING AT HOME

You will need:

- A dark-coloured bowl, preferably ceramic or metal
- 1 tsp olive oil
- Water (enough to fill your bowl)
- A candle
- Pen and paper

Method:

1. Fill your bowl with water and place it on a table.

2. Light the candle and dim the lights.

3. Take a few deep breaths and, when you feel ready, pour the olive oil into the water.

4. Write down or draw every shape you see using the space on the following page.

5. Read through the list of shapes you've jotted down and try to work out what each shape means for you. For example, animal symbolism is common in readings – a butterfly could signal that you are about to spread your wings while an elephant signifies wisdom and good luck.

What shapes do you see in the water? Draw or write them here.

Looking for the answer often teaches us more than finding it

AUGURY

In many spiritual circles, it is thought that birds bridge the gap between this world and the next, and that observing them closely can reveal the future. This lesser-known fortune-telling practice dates back thousands of years and was used by ancient Greeks, Romans, Egyptians, Celts and indigenous people of North America.

To tune into what birds might be trying to tell you, you need to become aware of them on a daily basis. Has an unusual bird visited your garden? Have you seen a flock of birds make a curious pattern in the sky? Or do you keep seeing the same species over and over again in different places?

Make a note of the type of birds you see, along with the date and how the experience made you feel. Do you know instinctively what message they were trying to convey?

Bird behaviour and meaning

Here are a few bird behaviours to look out for and their meanings:

Flying left to right –
your situation will improve quickly

Flying high and fast –
success is winging its way to you

Flying away from you –
your plans will be delayed

Flying against the wind –
someone in your life is not who they seem

NGGÀM

Nggàm is a method of divination found in western Cameroon that uses the movements of spiders or crabs to predict future events. It is most often performed using a type of tarantula that lives in burrows. Cards made from leaves marked with traditional symbols are scattered around the opening of the spider's burrow, covering the entrance. This prompts the creature to run out and investigate, dislodging cards as it moves. The pattern of cards left in the critter's wake is then interpreted for a reading. Land crabs are used in a similar fashion.

Tarantula burrows might be hard to come by, but if you see a spider in your home, it is a good omen – it means money is coming your way. Spy one in the morning and you will receive bad news, but spot one in the evening and it is a sign of luck. A spider crawling down the wall at night means trouble at work, and if it is crawling upward, a wish will be granted.

Nggàm at home

If you find a small spider in your home, ask it a question and gently place it on the grid below. Note the pictures it moves across. The more the spider visits an image, the better. If you don't have a spider to hand, spin a small coin on the picture and watch where it lands.

Life is like a web and you as a spider. All you need is time, energy and resources. Go, create it.

SACHIN CHOUDHARY

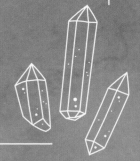

ASTROLOGY

Everybody has a star sign. Astrology is about much more than simply reading your daily horoscope; it is the study of the influence that the stars and planets have on your life. It is thought that the position of the planets at the time of your birth suggests your personality traits and can predict what your path through life is destined to be.

The birth of astrology as we know it today is attributed to the Babylonians, who used astrological charts to predict celestial events and then introduced the practice to the Greeks in the fourth century BCE. Back then it was taken very seriously, with the likes of Aristotle and Plato studying astrology as a science.

Identify your zodiac sign below

Aquarius
January 20–February 18

Pisces
February 19–March 20

Aries
March 21–April 19

Taurus
April 20–May 20

Gemini
May 21–June 20

Cancer
June 21–July 22

Leo
July 23–August 22

Virgo
August 23–September 22

Libra
September 23–October 22

Scorpio
October 23–November 21

Sagittarius
November 22–December 21

Capricorn
December 22–January 19

Star signs and character traits

Below are some of the main attributes of the 12 signs of the zodiac:

Aquarius – Daydreamers who are generally sensitive and kind.

Pisces – Imaginative and in touch with their spiritual nature.

Aries – Typically bold, adventurous and outspoken. Passionate and headstrong.

Taurus – Sensual and grounded. Love the finer things in life.

Gemini – Quick-witted social butterflies who can be indecisive.

Cancer – Calm, loving and enjoy home comforts.

Leo – Brave, attention-loving and loyal.

Virgo – Practical, grounded and sensible.

Libra – Romantics with a strong sense of justice.

Scorpio – Determined, obsessive and magnetic.

Sagittarius – Positive, spontaneous and communicative.

Capricorn – Hardworking, reliable and practical.

Create a birth chart

For a more in-depth look at how the stars are shaping your destiny, you can map a birth chart, which depicts exactly where the planets were in their journey around the sun at the moment you were born. There are many websites to help you map yours.

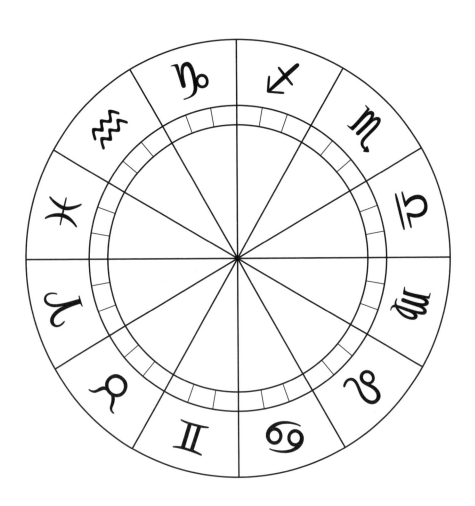

There is no better boat than a horoscope to help a man cross over the sea of life.

VARĀHAMIHIRA

TASSEOGRAPHY

The term tasseography comes from *tasso*, the Arabic word for cup, and the Greek *grapho*, which means writing. It therefore translates to "writing in a cup" and refers to the art of reading tea leaves.

In today's world, people don't drink loose-leaf tea like they used to, so tasseography isn't the popular pastime it once was. But it can still be performed with any remnants left at the bottom of a cup, such as hot chocolate or chai, though tea leaves are best.

HOW TO READ TEA

You will need:

- A teapot, a cup and a small plate
- Loose-leaf tea
- 1 cup of freshly boiled water
- Pen and paper

Method:

1. Make some loose-leaf tea in a pot, pour a cup and drink it until there is only a tiny bit of liquid left along with the tea leaves.

2. Close your eyes, swirl your cup and ask a question about your future.

3. Open your eyes, put the plate over the cup, tip both upside down and wait a few minutes.

4. Pick up the cup and look inside – what shapes have the tea leaves made? Are there any symbols? It is said that your unconscious mind, which knows your destiny, will have manifested the shapes you are meant to see.

Note the patterns or shapes you see at the bottom of your tea cup. Do they form any pictures? Use the chart below to identify the shapes.

**receptiveness,
introspection**

**unity,
purification**

**bringing
together**

good luck

**success,
new beginnings**

caution, stop

**creativity, time
for problem solving**

**travel,
change**

**excellence,
success**

SHUFFLEMANCY

Shufflemancy is a form of divination that uses songs in a playlist as a way of receiving messages. This may sound strange, but remember, the universe works in mysterious ways! Absolutely anything can be used to deliver a message. Music is actually the perfect tool, because it is a form of storytelling, and every song delivers its own message.

All you need to do is close your eyes, take a deep breath and ask a question. Then, using a computer, phone or any device that has a playlist, play a random song using the "shuffle" function.

As the song plays, consider how it makes you feel and whether it relates to the question you asked.

What is the meaning you've drawn from the name of the song/singer?

....

....

How does the song make you feel?

....

....

Do the lyrics relate to the question you asked?

....

....

Does the album art trigger any emotions?

....

....

When you're happy,
you enjoy the music,
but when you're sad, you
understand the lyrics.

FRANK OCEAN

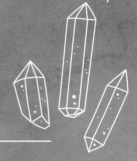

THE LAW OF ATTRACTION

The law of attraction, which is sometimes known as manifesting, is based on the notion that you send out an invisible message to the universe via your thoughts and emotions, which are then reflected back to you in the form of things, people or events. Some believe it is possible to attract success, wealth, health and happiness into your life through the power of thought alone.

It's not as easy as simply daydreaming your way to success, you have to feel it. So, if it is more money you want, you need to start behaving like a rich person. That doesn't mean running up an overdraft, it means generating a feeling of abundance within yourself. You might do this by treating yourself to something you have wanted for a while (if you can afford it), or appreciating how abundant your life already is, with a roof over your head, clothes on your back and food on the table.

Take the law of attraction quiz

Before you start attempting to manifest things into your life, it's wise first to try and work out what it is you really want. Take this quiz to discover what your heart desires most.

1. What's your dream holiday?

a) Somewhere hot and tropical
b) A staycation
c) An active outdoors holiday
d) There's no time for a holiday!

2. What would you do if you won the lottery?

a) Buy a sports car
b) Invest in property
c) Give money to family and friends
d) Bank it and vow not to change your spending habits

3. How is your career going?

a) Okay-ish
b) Great!
c) You want to change career path
d) You hate your job

4. Who is your dream romantic partner?

a) Someone rich
b) A nature lover
c) A keen athlete
d) An office worker

5. What makes you cry?

a) Household bills
b) Sad music
c) Another's pain
d) Not much, you hardly ever shed tears

The results

Mostly As: The finer things in life are important to you. Focus on what you have already rather than what you haven't, and the universe will send more your way.

Mostly Bs: Home comforts matter to you and you're content with life. This is the key to a happy future. Keep flexing your gratitude muscle.

Mostly Cs: You are an adventurer who values family and friends. Continue to spend time in nature as it is nourishing you.

Mostly Ds: You are stuck in a rut. Remember, you can do or be anything you want. Everything starts with a decision – make yours to create the life you crave.

Use this space to write down a list of things you would like to attract into your life:

....

....

....

....

....

....

....

....

....

....

....

....

True manifesting is allowing the universe to catch up with your dreams.

GABRIELLE BERNSTEIN

CRYSTAL BALL GAZING

Also known as crystallomancy, the art of crystal ball gazing is a familiar image associated with end-of-pier fortune tellers. In reality, it is one of the oldest forms of divination and was practised by ancient civilizations. It is thought that staring into a crystal ball can awaken psychic abilities.

Crystal ball gazing is a form of scrying, which can also be done with a mirror, a pool of water, precious stones or any other transparent object. It is said to be most powerful when practised by the light of a full moon.

How to use a crystal ball to predict your future

If you are lucky enough to own a crystal ball, try awakening your psychic abilities using the method below.

1. Place your crystal ball on a stand.

2. Gaze into it, focusing deeply and in silence.

3. Allow your mind to wander.

4. Relax. You might see images appear before your eyes – they may look like wisps of smoke inside the ball.

Write down everything you saw below.

....

....

....

....

....

....

....

Your self-worth
is determined by you.
You don't have to depend
on someone else telling
you who you are.

BEYONCÉ

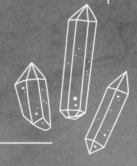

Mirror scrying

If you don't own or don't want to purchase a crystal ball, you can also practise scrying with a mirror.

1. Dim the lights and gaze at your reflection in a mirror.

2. Take some deep breaths, clear your mind and relax.

3. Try and look beyond the mirror's surface, as if you were staring into a tunnel.

4. Ask your question out loud.

5. Keep looking into the mirror and allow shapes, symbols or colours to emerge.

Are there any symbols, animals, plants, etc. that you can make out?

Images may form outside the edge of the mirror. Take a deep breath and allow them to emerge.

YOU HAVE THE POWER WITHIN YOU TO BELIEVE IN YOURSELF

LITHOMANCY

Lithomancy is the practice of predicting the future using stones or crystals. It comes from the Greek words *lithos*, which means stone, and *manteia*, which translates to divination. Records show that lithomancy goes back as far as the late 800s CE.

You simply plunge your hand into a bag full of crystals or stones and remove a fistful, then see if there is any symbolism or meaning in those you have chosen. It works best when you use a range of crystals that have varying properties. You can use any small objects, such as shells or beads, so long as you assign a meaning to each of them.

For a deeper lithomancy reading

Take a piece of paper and label it with sections such as "yes", "no", "work", "love", "health", etc. Then take a handful of crystals or stones from a bag and cast them onto the paper as if you were throwing dice. Make your predictions according to where the crystals have landed.

Crystals and their symbolism

For a rounded lithomancy reading, invest in some crystals with varying properties and meanings, such as:

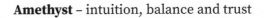

Amethyst – intuition, balance and trust

Moonstone – sensuality and travel

Lapis Lazuli – wisdom and truth

Clear Quartz – awareness, energy and clarity of thought

Rose Quartz – love, healing and compassion

Citrine – joy and abundance

Aventurine – prosperity and luck

Red Jasper – strength and stability

Labradorite – truth and nobility

Positivity is a

superpower

JOURNALING

Journaling is the process of writing down your thoughts and feelings without censoring yourself. If you do this daily, you'll get an overview of how you have reacted to various events in your life, and it will help when it comes to mapping out your future.

Journaling can be a meditative process that can help process feelings – putting them on a page makes it easier to stand back and examine them.

If you want to be creative, use coloured pens, stickers and sketches to illustrate your journal. You can also pepper it with statements or quotes that inspire you. Many people like to write on their phones, but by using pen and paper you can go much deeper. It is good to have a screen break, and you won't be distracted by incoming messages.

Practise journaling by writing your thoughts below:

Stream of consciousness journaling

Stream of consciousness journaling is a different and more insightful take on journaling. It is the practice of writing your thoughts as they come to you with no planning, stopping or editing. It usually works best first thing in the morning.

The minute you wake up, pick up a pen or pencil and write without thinking too much about what you're writing. Keep the pen moving. If you can't think of anything to say, write "I am writing" repeatedly and soon you will be jotting down varied sentences at speed.

It is a bit like a brain dump. Get rid of any clutter in your mind and you'll feel clear-headed afterward. It is also an excellent way to tap into the unconscious mind. Often, when you look back at your words, you will see truths about your life that you haven't yet admitted to yourself. It can be a really illuminating process.

It is vital that your journal remains private. The words inside are not for anyone else's eyes. Worrying about another person reading them will inhibit the process. Once you've read over your writing, you can tear it up, burn it or hide it in a safe place.

Practise some stream of consciousness writing below:

A word after a word
after a word is power.

MARGARET ATWOOD

BRONTOMANCY

Brontomancy describes the practice of fortune telling using thunderstorms and stems from the Greek words *bronto*, which means thunder and *mancy*, which translates to prophecy. The interpretation depends on the volume of thunder, direction and length.

You don't need any special tools to do this, just follow the guide below:

Thunder on Monday – a woman will be leaving your life

Thunder on Tuesday and Thursday – abundance

Thunder on Wednesday – trouble lies ahead

Thunder on Friday – great suffering, tragedy

Thunder on Saturday – illness could be in store

Thunder on Sunday – a man of authority is departing

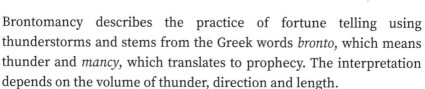

RUNES

Rune casting has a long history and involves casting stones with ancient letters on them. As they land, they form random patterns, which you can interpret by looking at the meaning of each letter.

The term "runes" comes from the ancient Norse word *run* and can be translated as "magic sign". The runes themselves use an alphabet employed long before the Latin alphabet, which only became prominent in the late Middle Ages.

There are 24 runes in a set, which are usually made of wood, stones or crystals. You can buy ready-made runes, or you can make your own by carving or painting the letters onto the materials of your choice. It is said that if you cast runes that are made by your own hand, they will be imbued with even more magic.

CASTING THE RUNES

You will need:

- 24 rune pieces
- A small bag
- A small white cloth
- Notepad and pen

Method:

1. Place the white cloth on the table. Take a deep breath, close your eyes and put your hand into the bag of runes.

2. Mix the runes as you ask a question – it doesn't necessarily require a simple "yes" or "no" answer.

3. Shake the bag, take out a handful of runes and cast them over the white cloth. Any that land off the cloth shouldn't be counted as part of your reading.

4. Note down the runes that have landed for you and look at the various meanings of each one on the following page. Take your time to interpret the message. If nothing springs to mind immediately, go back to your notes a day or so later and things might seem clearer then.

Runes and their meanings

Fehu – fresh start, wealth

Uruz – strength

Thurisaz – chaos and conflict

Ansuz – inspiration and communication

Raidho – journeys and leadership

Kenaz – a guiding light

Cebo – partnership

Wunjo – joy

Hagalaz – divine intervention

Nauthiz – restriction

Isa – stillness

Jera – divine timing

Eihwaz – perseverance

Perthro – rebirth

Algiz – divine protection

Solwilo – completion

Tiwaz – victory

Berkano – growth

Ehwaz – moving on

Mannaz – image

Laguz – health

Inguz – fertility

Othala – separation

Dagaz – insight

YOU ARE
THE MAGIC
YOU SEEK

TAROT

Tarot is a form of fortune telling that is done using a deck of 78 cards. You don't need any training or special powers to do it – all you need is a set of tarot cards, which are easy to come by and inexpensive.

The tarot deck consists of 22 major arcana cards, which represent the themes in your life, and 56 minor arcana cards, which describe situations, help you make choices and reflect your state of mind.

When you first get your tarot deck, take some time to familiarize yourself with it. Look at the images and descriptions. Think about how each of them makes you feel. You should not take the meaning of the cards literally – for example, some people panic when they draw the Death card, but it can mean rebirth and the start of a new phase in your life.

Common tarot cards and their meaning

Major arcana

The Tower – Unexpected change. Reversed, a fear of change.

The Wheel of Fortune – The passage of time and good luck. Reversed and you are not in control of your life.

The World – Freedom and achievement. Reversed signals emptiness and stagnation.

The Lovers – Harmony and attraction. Reversed could be a warning to think carefully about your choices.

Minor arcana

There are four suits of minor arcana. They are:

   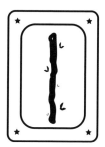

Cups – Relationships, emotions and desires

Swords – Thoughts, ideas and conflict

Pentacles – Possessions, money and career

Wands – Energy, spirituality and growth

The numbers on the cards mean the following:

1 – Ace, new beginnings

2 – Growth

3 – Stability

4 – Challenge

5 – Triumph

6 – Choices

7 – Movement

8 – Attainment

9 – Completion

Tarot reading

To perform a tarot reading, prepare a sacred space, using whatever items make you feel calm and energized. Candles, flowers, scented oils and a tablecloth could be used.

It's best to start with a three-card reading. When you are ready, close your eyes, take a deep breath and shuffle the cards. Deal three cards in front of you in a row, face-up. The first card you draw (on the left) will represent the past, the second (in the middle) is the present, and the third (on the right) represents the future. If they are upside down, they are "reversed" so you'll have to consider the opposite of what the card means.

Start by looking at the central, "present" card, then move to the past and finally take in the right-hand card, which is your future. When you have considered what each card means separately, think about how they flow together as one answer.

*Tarot reading is an
art based on intuition,
interpretation,
and perception.*

NIKITA DUDANI

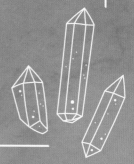

PENDULUM

A pendulum is a weighted object, such as a crystal or piece of stone, which hangs from a cord or chain. It is said to act as a transmitter of energy and will move independently when you ask it a question with a "yes" or "no" answer. The pendulum is perfect if you are looking for a quick answer to a pressing problem.

You can use any object that isn't magnetic to make a pendulum, or you can easily buy them ready-made, relatively cheaply. Crystals are considered the most effective material.

To use the pendulum, sit in a quiet room, close your eyes and centre yourself. Hold the pendulum by the cord in front of you, keeping your arm straight. It will either move from side to side or in a circle. Decide which movement represents each answer.

DACTYLOMANCY

Dactylomancy is a form of divination that is performed using a ring. The ring is suspended on a chain or piece of string and hung above a board or items of meaning, just like a pendulum. In Europe, during the Middle Ages, a common practice was to use a board marked with the symbols of the zodiac.

Discs representing each letter of the alphabet were placed on the table. The ring was suspended on a piece of string, which was burned until the ring fell. The reading was based on where the ring landed.

Using a ring pendulum is also a common way of trying to find out the sex of an unborn child. It is said that if the ring moves back and forth, it's a boy, and if it moves in a circular motion, the baby is a girl. Traditionally, the ring used for this method should belong to the mother of the child.

Try dactylomancy

Place a ring on a chain or string (it is best to use a ring that you wear on a daily basis). Clear your mind and hold the ring pendulum over the board on the following page. Ask a question and slowly move the ring across the letters on the board, from left to right. If it starts to move independently over a particular letter, write it down. Are any words forming? If it appears to be a jumble of letters, is there an anagram that suddenly seems obvious to you?

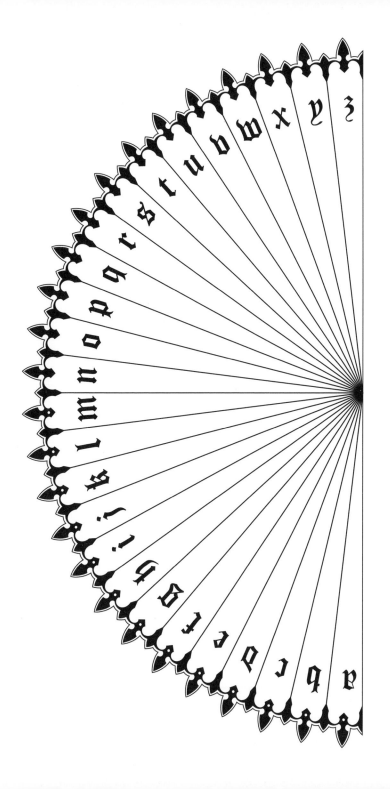

You are

divine

RHABDOMANCY

Also known as dowsing, this method of divination was commonly used to find sources of water using L-shaped sticks, known as rods. It is thought to have originated in sixteenth-century Germany. Today, you can also use this method to find a lost item.

You'll need either two L-shaped dowsing rods, or you can use one Y-shaped stick. Go into the room where you suspect the item might be and hold your sticks at arm's length a couple of inches apart. With a Y-shaped stick, hold each end of the Y with one hand. Ask the rods to find your missing possession while walking slowly around the room. When they start to twitch, search the area and hopefully you'll find what you are looking for.

MAKE YOUR OWN DOWSING RODS

You will need:

- Two wire coat hangers
- A pair of pliers
- Wire cutters
- Two plastic ballpoint pens

Method:

1. Using the pliers for grip if you need to, untwist the hooks of the hangers so that you are left with two lengths of wire. Straighten the wires and cut off the twisted ends.

2. Turn each piece of wire into an L-shape with a 90-degree angle.

3. Remove the ink cartridges from the ballpoint pens and place the "handles" of the rods inside the hollow plastic tube.

4. Poke a short length of wire through the tip of the ballpoint pen casing and fold it, so that it stays in place. Your rods are now ready to use!

YOU ARE WORTHY OF LIVING THE LIFE OF YOUR DREAMS

NAEVIOLOGY

Naeviology refers to the practice of fortune telling using marks on the body, such as moles, birthmarks, freckles and scars. It was hugely popular in the eighteenth and nineteenth centuries and has roots in Chinese astrology, which believes that moles represent certain characteristics and can appear on the body in response to events in our lives. The word "naeviology" comes from the Latin *naevus*, which means mole or birthmark.

Have a go at naeviology

Note any markings and their position on your own body and then check their meanings according to naeviology.

Forehead	centre: difficulty in communicating with authority
	side: driven
Eyebrows	underneath: sudden wealth
	above: a steady flow of cash
Cheeks	right cheek: strong feelings
	left cheek: financial difficulties
Ears	earlobe: good reputation
	inside ear: intelligence
Nose	end of nose: relationship trouble
	side: good with money
Lips	upper lip: enjoy the finer things in life
	bottom: successful children
Neck	back of neck: career success
	front: energetic
Arms	below elbow: compassionate
	above elbow: attracts money easily
Chest	career success
Hands	skilled at using your hands
Legs	thighs: high sex drive
	calf: burnout
	knees: financial success
Feet	leadership and a love of travel

Use this outline to mark the locations of any marks on your body.

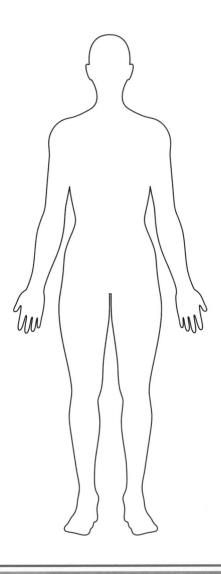

There are beautiful
moments of magic
in everyone's life.

PENÉLOPE CRUZ

CARTOMANCY

Cartomancy encapsulates any form of divination using cards, for example tarot, but you can use any deck of cards, even a standard pack of 52 playing cards. Here are the meanings of the cards in a deck of ordinary playing cards:

Spades represent struggles or challenges.
2 – A tough choice
3 – Bad news
4 – Rewards
5 – A new venture
6 – Stop spending
7 – Friendship
8 – A big decision
9 – A friend or family member starts a new chapter
10 – Stay positive
Jack – People are holding you back
Queen – Be wary of a woman in a position of power
King – Be wary of a male boss at work
Ace – A door closes

Hearts represent emotions and relationships with others.
2 – Don't take your partner for granted
3 – Embrace commitment
4 – Your relationship looks bright. If you are single, love is on its way
5 – Home life is about to change
6 – Teamwork is the key to success
7 – Don't hold grudges
8 – Say "yes" more often
9 – Your relationship will soon progress
10 – Good news is coming
Jack – Build bridges with a friend

Queen – Talk to your mother or mother figure
King – Your dad or father figure wants to talk to you
Ace – Something new and exciting lies ahead

Clubs represent positive change.
2 – Stay in touch with friends
3 – Believe in your creative ability
4 – Step out of your comfort zone
5 – Do that thing you've always talked about
6 – Listen to your gut instinct
7 – Be open with a partner or friend
8 – Spend time meditating
9 – A new phase is about to begin
10 – You're going on a journey
Jack – Be honest with others
Queen – A charismatic woman will enter your life
King – You will meet a generous man
Ace – Learn something new

Diamonds represent money and finances.
2 – Your finances will improve
3 – Don't argue over money
4 – Look after your money
5 – You will get some news that impacts finances
6 – Start budgeting
7 – Choose investments wisely
8 – Money is on its way
9 – Save for a future expense
10 – Work hard and you'll reap the rewards
Jack – Someone close has unfortunate financial news
Queen – A woman who loves to spend enters your life
King – You will meet a male entrepreneur
Ace – Take advantage of upcoming important news

How to read a deck of playing cards

Reading playing cards is similar to tarot. It's not about taking the meaning of each card literally, but about looking at the spread of cards and seeing how they might relate to your life circumstances.

It's best to use a new pack of cards that haven't been touched yet by others. Open the pack and cleanse the cards using a crystal – rose quartz is good for this – simply lay the crystal on top of the deck and leave it for a couple of hours.

When you are ready to do a reading, shuffle the cards with a question in mind. Deal three cards and lay them face up. Like before, the first card is the past, the second is the present, and the third represents the future. Look up the meaning of each card and then take some time to see how they relate to your current situation.

It's not about the hand you're dealt; it's how you play the game that counts

TYROMANCY

Derived from the Greek words *turos* (cheese) and *mantaeia* (divination), tyromancy is the art of fortune telling using cheese. In the Middle Ages, the shape of a piece of cheese, patterns made by the holes and how mould grew on it, were all seen as omens.

It was traditional for single women to write the names of all their prospective partners on pieces of cheese – the bit that grew mould first would indicate who was the perfect soulmate. Fortune tellers also looked for symbols in cheese curds as they coagulated to form cheese.

You might see tyromancy as a waste of good cheese, but if you'd like to try it, simply ask a question and write the possible answers on chunks of hard cheese. Put them in a small plastic tub and leave at the back of the fridge until one of them shows signs of mould and gives you the answer.

CROMNIOMANCY

Cromniomancy is the art of fortune telling using onions (the word *cromnion* means onion in Greek) and was popular across Europe, Africa and northern Asia where the onion was seen as a symbol of spirituality in ancient cultures.

There are a number of cromniomancy methods. The most popular is to inscribe onions with names as a way of finding out information about absent friends and loved ones. Names are etched into individual onions, which are then left to sprout. The quicker the onion is to grow green shoots, the healthier the person whose name is it bears.

Another method is to place 12 onions in a row, representing the months of the year. A pinch of salt is sprinkled onto each and they are left overnight. The amount of moisture collected in each onion signals how much rain could be expected throughout the year.

It is also believed that wishes will come true when onion skins are burned on a fire.

PHRENOLOGY

Phrenology uses the measurements of your skull to determine what character traits and abilities you are likely to possess. It was a popular medical practice in the late nineteenth century, though it was considered controversial, even by scholars, as it was often used to justify racism, sexism and classism.

It is based on the work of a German physician called Franz Joseph Gall who mapped out the regions of the brain that correspond to 26 organs. These were then assigned personality traits, such as cautiousness, generosity and memory. Practitioners would feel the head and identify any bumps, which were then "read" using Gall's map of the skull.

Today, phrenology is no longer used in medicine, but it has gained popularity as a form of divination. Followers perform a cold reading by feeling a person's skull, then give an interpretation of health, character and temperament.

A simple guide to phrenology

Using your fingers, carefully examine your own head and feel for any bumps. If you find any, mark them on the pictures below. When you've finished, you can read your skull using the phrenology map overleaf.

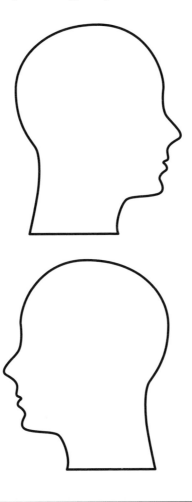

Phrenology map

Referring to your illustrations, interpret the shape of your own skull using the phrenology map below.

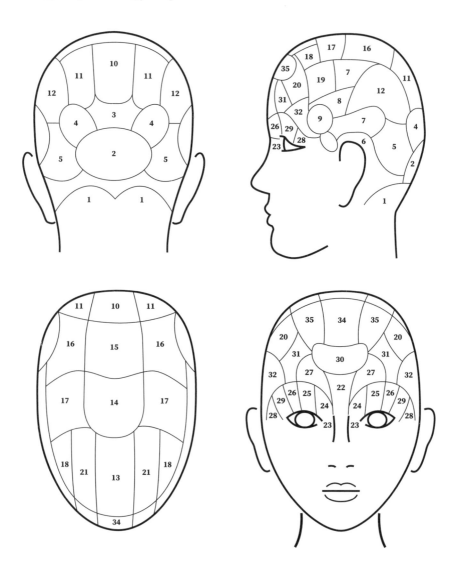

1. Amativeness
2. Philoprogenitiveness
3. Inhabitiveness
4. Adhesiveness
5. Combativeness
6. Destructiveness
7. Secretiveness
8. Acquisitiveness
9. Constructiveness
10. Self-esteem
11. Love of approbation
12. Cautiousness
13. Benevolence
14. Veneration
15. Firmness
16. Conscientiousness
17. Hope
18. Wonder

19. Ideality
20. Wit
21. Imitation
22. Individuality
23. Form
24. Size
25. Weight
26. Colouring
27. Locality
28. Number
29. Order
30. Eventuality
31. Time
32. Tune
33. Language
34. Comparison
35. Causality

CONCHOMANCY

Conchomancy is a method of fortune telling using sea shells – cowrie shells were often used, as ancient tribes considered them to be "the mouthpiece" of God.

The simplest method of conchomancy is to use a single shell, preferably one with a flat side. First, you'll need to cleanse it. Traditionally, this involves laying the shell on a plate of salt on a windowsill where it will be bathed in the light of the full moon.

Once cleansed, hold the shell in your hands and ask a question that requires a "yes" or "no" answer. Decide which side of the shell represents "yes" and "no", hold it in front of your heart for a few seconds and then toss it gently onto a cloth. Whichever side is face up gives your answer. You can use more than one shell, but make it an odd number, so you get a definitive answer.

Each day is like a newly discovered seashell. Treasure it and admire its beauty

NEPHOMANCY

Nephomancy is a type of divination that is based on the shape, position and colour of clouds in the sky. It comes from the Greek word *nephos,* which means cloud, and was used extensively by Celtic druids.

The best time to practise is when there are plenty of clouds to see and it's not raining. It's simple, all you need to do is lie on a blanket, relax and look up at the sky (making sure that you don't glance at the sun).

Try not to think too hard about it, just let the clouds drift by and then, when you see an image or something notable, record it in a notebook. Or, to avoid having to interrupt your viewing, you could dictate into your phone and listen back to the recording later. It is common to see faces in the clouds: note their expressions and how they make you feel. Animals also appear regularly. Horses, for example, suggest you should stick to your dreams and follow your heart in order to see your wishes come true.

*Be a rainbow in
someone else's cloud.*

MAYA ANGELOU .

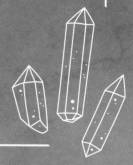

CHIROGNOMY

Chirognomy is an off-shoot of palmistry and uses the shape of the hands, fingers and nails as a method of analyzing a person's character traits. The texture of the skin and the fleshy mounds of the palm also play a part.

It is derived from the Greek words *chiro,* which means hand and *gnomonia,* which translates to judge. It dates back to the beginnings of palmistry in ancient India at around the fourth century BCE, but the first person to formulate a hand-shape classification bible was a Frenchman called Casimir Stanislas D'Arpentigny. He wrote the book *La Chirognomie,* which was published in 1839.

Strictly speaking, it isn't a method of divination, although if you understand your own character and behaviours, it is easier to predict the life choices and experiences you may face in the future.

Take the chirognomy quiz

Examine your palm on your dominant hand and pick the relevant description:

a) Short fingers and a longish palm

b) Square palm and short fingers

c) Long fingers and a square palm

d) Rectangular palm with long fingers

Analysis:

a) The Fire Hand. You're outgoing, sometimes controlling, occasionally hyper and emotional.

b) The Earth Hand. You dislike change, are an excellent worker and emotionally stable.

c) The Air Hand. You're a great communicator, a skilled writer, friendly and easily bored at times.

d) The Water Hand. You are artistic and often let your heart rule your head.

Chirognomy hand reading

Using the diagram below and the descriptions overleaf, take a look and see what your hands reveal about your personality.

In chirognomy, each finger is named after a planet – there's Jupiter, Saturn, Apollo, Mercury and Venus (the thumb).

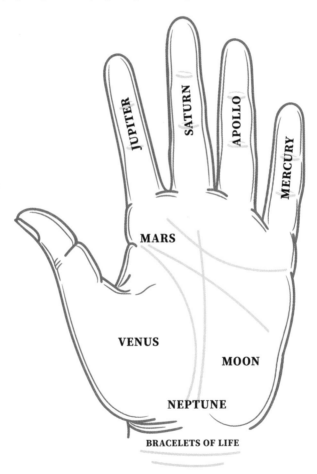

JUPITER

SATURN

APOLLO

MERCURY

MARS

VENUS

MOON

NEPTUNE

BRACELETS OF LIFE

Jupiter finger – When long, this finger shows confidence and leadership. Short and you're shy and unconfident.

Saturn finger – Short suggests carelessness, while a long finger shows a good work ethic.

Apollo finger – Long and you are highly creative. Short means practical and down to earth.

Mercury finger – Long is a sign of intelligence, success and good communication skills. Short indicates immaturity.

Venus – Flat and not too fleshy, you are a sensitive home lover. If it is big, you are affectionate.

Moon – Relates to the imagination. The larger it is, the more artistic and romantic you are.

Mars – Small and criss-crossed with fine lines means struggle. When large with deep lines, you're a hard worker.

Neptune – When prominent, you are highly creative. If a line runs into the fate line, you are destined for leadership.

Bracelets of life – Represent health and wealth. The deeper, the better.

IF YOUR HANDS
HOLD ONTO
FEAR, YOU
CANNOT GRASP
THE TRUE
WONDER OF
THE UNIVERSE

FORTUNE COOKIES

Who doesn't love cracking open a fortune cookie at the end of a meal to see what words of wisdom or prediction will be revealed? Although fortune cookies are synonymous with Chinese culture, it is thought that they originated in America, where they were called "fortune tea cakes". More than three billion fortune cookies are made each year, which proves just how popular they continue to be. They begin as round cookies that are folded over a slip of paper bearing a message.

I CHING

The *I Ching* (or *Yi Jing*) is the book of Chinese wisdom collated by sages and fortune tellers over a period of 2,500 years. It consists of a series of 64 shapes that are made of six lines, either broken or solid, in various combinations. The book explains the meaning behind the shapes that can be made, with all the possible six-line combinations.

When you consult the *I Ching*, you build your shape from the bottom up, line by line. The configuration of each line depends on the result of a "yes" or "no" question. You can do it by tossing coins, shells, or picking stones or beads from a bag. You draw each line until you have six piled on top of one another. You then consult the book of *I Ching* to find out what your shape means.

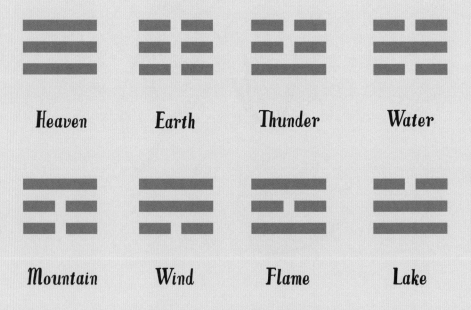

Heaven Earth Thunder Water

Mountain Wind Flame Lake

HOW TO DO AN *I CHING* READING

You will need:

- A notepad and pen
- Three coins

Method:

1. Ask a question. Shake the three coins and drop them on a table.

2. Draw your first hexagram line following the instructions below:

   - If you get three heads, draw a solid line and put an x by it: - x
   - Two heads and one tail is a broken line: - -
   - Two tails and one head is a solid line: —
   - Three tails is a broken line with an x: --x

3. Repeat this process another five times and build your shape from the bottom up.

4. Once you've completed all six lines, consult the book of *I Ching*.

Using beads for an *I Ching* reading

If drawing shapes based on "yes" or "no" feels too time consuming, you can also do a simple *I Ching* reading using beads. You'll need 16 in total, in four different colours, for example black, orange, white and red. They should all be the same shape and size and should be divided into the following:

- Seven white beads: --
- Five orange beads: –
- Three red beads: -x
- One black bead: --x

Each bead represents an *I Ching* line. Place the beads in a bag or bowl, close your eyes and pick one out. Draw the line that it represents. Repeat this six times, adding the new lines on top of the previous one until you have created a shape. You can then look up their meaning in the book of *I Ching*.

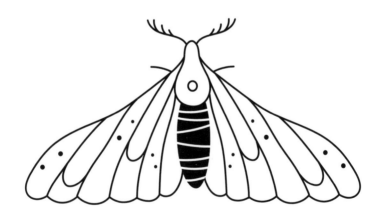

Genius is the ability to
receive from the universe.

I CHING

CAPNOMANCY

Capnomancy is a method of divination that interprets the shapes and patterns of smoke as it rises from a fire and is believed to have originated in ancient Babylon, where, on certain days, sages would burn cedar branches and analyze the resulting smoke.

Another capnomancy method was to throw jasmine, poppy seeds or granulated incense onto a fire and inhale the smoke as a means of getting rid of bad omens. In many cultures, it was thought that smoke possessed magical properties, so it was often used in rituals and ceremonies.

How to read smoke from a fire

Thin smoke moving to the right – good fortune is on its way

Smoke blown back by a breeze – a bad omen

Low-hanging smoke – a storm is brewing

Smudging

Smudging is a term used to describe the burning of sage, which is an ancient ritual used for cleansing and healing. It involves bunching dried sage together, burning it and wafting the smoke to remove any bad energy in the room. It can be burned in a bowl or tied to form a smudging stick. Though sage is the traditional ingredient, a range of herbs can be used in smudging, and you should choose the one that best fits your intention. Before you begin, set your intention, remove pets and anything highly flammable from the room and make sure you fan the smoke into every corner. Always take care when using fire for rituals. If you see embers dropping to the ground, put them out immediately.

Smudging herbs and their uses

Clove – prevents the spread of gossip

Mint – increases libido

Sage – protects against evil

Rose – encourages prophetic dreams

African violet – encourages spirituality in the home

Basil – gets rid of unwanted ghosts

Sweetgrass – attracts positive energy

Behold, how great
a matter a little
fire kindleth!

SAINT JAMES THE JUST

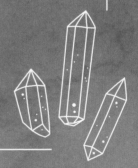

FAVOMANCY

Favomancy is a method of fortune telling that involves casting a handful of beans and interpreting the patterns they make when they land. Legend has it that this method of divination is even older than tarot.

The term is derived from the Latin words *Vicia faba*, which means fava or broad bean. This method of divination was popular among Islamic groups in Russia centuries ago, and it is still practised by seers there today. In Bosnia and Herzegovina, fortune tellers who use favomancy are referred to as bean-throwers. A similar method of divination exists in Iran, which uses peas in place of beans.

It's a simple technique that anyone can do. You can use any beans, as long as they are dry – you can even use buttons or small coins. A full favomancy set consists of 41 beans, which should all be a similar size and look as identical as possible.

Simple favomancy reading

The simplest form of favomancy is to ask a "yes" or "no" question using three beans. Mark one side of each bean with an X using a pen, shake them in your hands as you would a set of dice and cast them onto a soft cloth on a table. If three beans lie with the X face up it's a definite "no", two is "maybe", one is "unlikely" and if none show the X, then it's an absolute "yes"!

Interpreting favomancy images

You can also use beans as a tool for scrying. Take a bag of 41 beans, shake them up and cast them all onto a cloth. Close your eyes, take a deep breath and then look at the beans. Do any shapes pop out at you? If they do, make a note and see if they relate to your life situation.

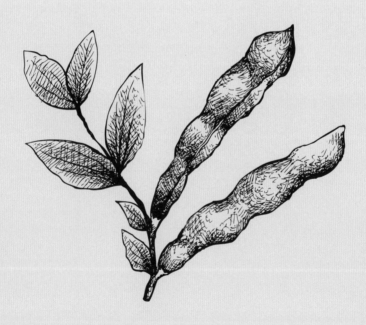

READING BEANS WITH A FORTUNE-TELLING SQUARE

You can also use the beans in conjunction with a fortune-telling square (overleaf).

You will need:

- 41 identical beans
- A notebook and pen
- The grid overleaf

Method:

1. Shuffle the beans and divide them into three random piles (don't count them).

2. Divide the first pile into groups of four until you only have between one and four beans left. Place those remaining beans in the top-left square.

3. Do the same with the next pile of beans, placing the remaining beans on the top-middle square.

4. Repeat the process, continuing to move left to right, from the top row to the bottom. The more beans there are on a square, the more significance it has on your life.

5. Take some time to analyze the results. Jot down any thoughts and see how the results come together as a whole.

love	money	career
travel	friendship	magic
home	health	happiness

Conjure the
magic inside you

APANTOMANCY

Apantomancy refers to a method of divination that is done by analyzing things that you happen upon by chance, particularly animals. It was used in ancient Rome, though the term comes from the Greek word *apantomai*, which means "to meet".

We all use this method without realizing – how many times have you seen a black cat and viewed it as a sign of good or bad luck, depending on where you live? Or worried when you've spied a solitary magpie?

Animals have been used in apantomancy for millenia – bats, cats, dogs, snakes and many more have all been assigned various omens. Spotting an owl can mean that a life-changing event is on the horizon, while a bluebird signals happy times ahead. When a dog follows a young woman home it is supposed to mean that a romantic relationship is imminent.

Animals that are a sign of good luck – goat, white horse, swallow, bats, deer, dog, elephant, fox

Animals that bring bad omens – donkey, raven, rabbit, bear, coyote, vulture, buzzard, white buffalo, cockerel

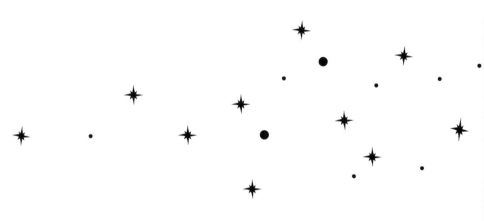

Some people talk to
animals. Not many listen
though. That's the problem.

A. A. MILNE

CLEDONOMANCY

Cledonomancy or cledonism refers to fortune telling by looking into the meaning of chance encounters – it can be words you hear often, repeated numbers or a person who shows up or calls just as you were thinking about them. It comes from the word *kledon,* which means "omen".

It was a popular method of divination in ancient Greece where both cledonism and apantomancy were viewed as communication from the gods. In Homer's *Odyssey,* Odysseus asks the gods for a sign and interprets a thunderclap as an answer from Zeus.

Cledonism is difficult to plan or predict as you will come across these signs when you least expect them. The next time you hear a song with lyrics that relate to something happening in your own life or keep being bombarded with the same word or phrase, take it as a sign that the universe is whispering in your ear.

THE UNIVERSE IS ALWAYS TRYING TO GET YOUR ATTENTION

DICE ROLLING

This method of fortune telling involves throwing an ordinary six-sided die and interpreting the resulting numbers.

In addition to playing dice, you can also use astragalomancy dice, which have both numbers and letters on them. This form of fortune telling is thousands of years old. Originally it would have been performed using small animal bones, most commonly the knucklebones. Dice were thrown against large, flat stones or animal skins, but for modern purposes, you can cast them onto any flat surface.

Simple dice divination

Hold two six-sided dice in your hands. Close your eyes and think of a pressing question. Roll the dice onto a flat surface and refer to the interpretations below to get your answer:

2 – No

3 – A nice surprise lies ahead

4 – You are about to get lucky

5 – A wish will come true

6 – Stay alert and you will find your answer

7 – A win is on the cards

8 – You already know the answer

9 – It's in the hands of fate

10 – Success is on its way

11 – The universe has your back

12 – Tranquillity will come into your life

Three-dice reading

To perform a more complex reading, use three dice. Ideally, they will be different colours as they'll represent the past, present and future. Cast them and refer to the following meanings:

Die 1: the past

1 – Complications lie ahead

2 – Something will come to an end

3 – An important message will arrive

4 – Good luck is coming your way

5 – You will achieve your goals

6 – You need to be vigilant

Die 2: the present

1 – Enthusiasm breeds success

2 – New ideas will be a boost

3 – Love will fill your life

4 – Arguments are likely

5 – An important event is on the cards

6 – A stranger disrupts your life

Die 3: the future

1 – Be careful for the sake of your health

2 – Try and avoid mistakes as things move quickly

3 – Muster up the energy to achieve your dreams

4 – Keep an eye out for new opportunities

5 – Celebrations are on the horizon

6 – Money will arrive soon

One who doesn't throw the dice, can never expect to score a six.

NAVJOT SINGH SIDHU

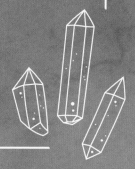

BELLOMANCY

Bellomancy is an ancient form of fortune telling that uses arrows to predict the future. It was used by the Babylonians, Greeks and Arabs.

Arrows were marked with possible answers to a question, for example, "God wants me to do it", "God forbids it", with a third remaining blank. The practitioner would then fire the arrows, and the one that went the furthest would provide an answer. If the blank arrow flew furthest, there would be another attempt. Sometimes arrows were plucked from a sleeve bearing various messages. It worked a bit like a lucky dip – whichever arrow was picked would provide the answer to a question.

We don't recommend buying a set of arrows to do this, but you could use a children's bow and arrow set, marking the arrows with "yes" or "no" answers. Or, you could mark tennis balls, or something similar, and the one you throw the farthest bears your answer.

Follow your own arrow

XYLOMANCY

Xylomancy is an ancient form of divination using sticks or pieces of wood. It features in the *Harry Potter* books as part of the divination curriculum. The term is derived from the Greek words *xylo* and *mantaeia*, which mean wood and divination.

In Slovenia, messages are read into the patterns that fallen pieces of wood make along a person's path, and in ancient times, if a tree limb fell suddenly, it meant that there was a surprise in store.

Later on, as xylomancy developed, small twigs were cast onto the ground and the shapes they made were interpreted.

How to read trees and twigs

Go for a walk in the woods or a forest and think about a situation you would like help with. Keep it in mind while being observant. Do you see any shapes or patterns in the trees around you? Do they remind you of anything? It could be that a bough looks as if it is about to break off or there are twigs on the floor that have fallen to form an arrow. Familiarize yourself with the runes on pages 60 and 61; do any of the twigs you see form these letters?

Casting twigs

Gather a pile of at least ten twigs of roughly equal size and strip the bark from them. Centre yourself, ask a question and throw them onto the ground. Look carefully at the way they have fallen. Have they formed any shapes? Can you see letters? Or runes?

Time spent
amongst trees is
never time wasted.

KATRINA MAYER

OVOMANCY

Ovomancy is a term used to describe divination by eggs and was popular in ancient Greece and Rome. It was often used as a way to try and determine the sex, health and characteristics of an unborn child in the womb. An egg would be rubbed on the pregnant mother's belly and then cracked into a dish. One yolk meant she was having one child, while two signalled twins. If the egg contained specks of blood, this was taken as a bad omen.

Another method of ovomancy involved hard-boiling an egg and writing "yes" and "no" on opposite sides. It was then rolled down a hill and the message was interpreted by looking at which way up it had landed and in which direction it was pointing.

EASY OVOMANCY

You can use eggs for divination purposes at any time, and this simple method can produce surprising results.

You will need:

- A chicken egg
- Bowl
- Cold water
  (enough to fill your bowl)
- A candle

Method:

1. Fill the bowl with water, light the candle and relax.

2. Run the egg over your body, keeping your question in mind.

3. Crack the egg into the water and watch as the egg white rises to the surface. Take note of the patterns and shapes it forms.

4. Look at the shell. If there are lots of cracks near the top, you will receive a positive outcome, but if the bottom bears more cracks, then you may not get the result you were hoping for.

ENJOY THE LITTLE THINGS IN LIFE

NUMEROLOGY

Everyone has a lucky number and we all get a tingle down the spine when the clock shows 11:11. Welcome to the world of numerology, the practice of studying the spiritual meaning of numbers. The idea that certain numbers are significant is held across the world. In Christianity, there is the holy trinity, while 666 is the mark of the devil. Hanukkah lasts for eight nights and in China the number four is unlucky, while eight brings good fortune.

What do numbers mean?

In numerology, the numbers one to nine have significant meanings, and if you see or experience them a lot, it could be a good sign.

1 – Independence and a taste for adventure

2 – Compassion and sensitivity

3 – Optimism and wit

4 – Hard work and organization

5 – Adventure and freedom

6 – Beauty and understanding

7 – Knowledge and spirituality

8 – Money and success

9 – Healing

Use numerology to work out your destiny

To find out what your path in life is, add up all the numbers in your date of birth, until you reach a single digit. For example, 23 March 1995 would equate to 2+3+3+1+9+9+5, giving you a total of 32. Next add 3+2 and your number is 5. (Any combinations that total 10 become 1.)

Work out your destiny number below:

Your destiny number:

1   **The leader** – You are destined to take the lead.
2   **The peacemaker** – Creating harmony is your superpower.
3   **The creative** – Your destiny is to express your true self.
4   **The teacher** – The next generation needs your wisdom.
5   **The adventurer** – Exploring is your calling.
6   **The carer** – You were born to take care of those you love.
7   **The researcher** – Focus on making new discoveries.
8   **The entrepreneur** – You are the boss of your own life.
9   **The giver** – You make the world a better place.

Number rules
the universe.

PYTHAGORAS

HEPTOMOLOGY

The number seven is so special, it has a type of divination of its own, called heptomology. The word *hepto* means seven in Greek, and *logy* represents the study of a particular topic. Heptomology is the practice of predicting future events using the number seven.

Mathematically, it's a special number. Seven is a prime number and has a whole list of properties not shared by other single digits.

It is also considered a lucky number in many religions. In the Old Testament, there are the seven days of creation, the feast of Passover lasts seven days and King David had seven brothers. In Hinduism, there are seven worlds in the universe and seven layers of the Earth, and in Judaism, seven blessings are given at a wedding.

If you come across the number seven, consider it a sign of good luck. The more you hone your intuition, the more likely you are to come across lucky number seven.

And one man in his
time plays many parts,
His acts being seven ages.

WILLIAM SHAKESPEARE

PSYCHOMETRY

Psychometry is the art of reading an object by tuning into the vibrations that have been left by its owner, like a kind of spiritual fingerprint. It is sometimes known as clairtangency, psychoscopy or token-object reading. It's a powerful way of strengthening your psychic abilities, and it can give insights into your family if you tap the energy of heirlooms.

The term comes from the Greek word *psyche* which means soul, and *metron*, meaning measure. It was coined in 1842 by American professor of physiology, Joseph Rodes Buchanan, who experimented with the technique, asking students to work out which drug was in a glass vial by holding it and using their intuitive capabilities.

Later a geologist called William F. Denton tried the technique using geological specimens. He wrapped them in a cloth and his sister Ann then held them against her forehead. The mental images she received enabled her to accurately identify the objects.

Have a go at psychometry

You don't need any special skills to be able to use psychometry, and the more you practise, the more attuned you'll become to the vibrations of the objects you use.

1. Ask a friend to bring you an object you know nothing about – it is best if this is something they have owned for a long time and use a lot.

2. Sit in a quiet room where you won't be disturbed.

3. Close your eyes and hold the object in your hands.

4. Take some deep breaths and wait for any images, emotions, sounds or information to come into your mind – don't dismiss a single thought.

5. Speak with the owner of the item about what you are experiencing to see if they can relate to your impressions. Don't worry about feeling silly – it's the things that you say without thinking too much that are likely to be revealing.

6. Return the object to its owner and record your reading, then ask the owner of the object if they recognize anything in what you've said.

You are a
powerful creator

PRECOGNITION

Precognition refers to the ability to predict an event before it actually happens. It often occurs in flashes of information that come in dreams or as sudden feelings that appear as if from nowhere. The term comes from the Latin *prior,* which means "prior to" and *cognito,* which translates as "to gain knowledge".

This was a common type of divination in ancient times, when prophets and seers were frequently consulted for their apparent abilities to predict the future.

Some people are born with precognitive ability and, like all spiritual techniques, it is something that can be honed and improved with practice. Research has found that most events that are predicted using this technique happen in a short time frame and involve a partner, family member or close friend. Only 15–25 per cent of precognitive predictions relate to strangers.

Do you have precognitive abilities?

Take our quiz to find out if you have the ability to predict the future.

Which of the following best describes your dreams?

a) So vivid that you can remember them when you wake up
b) Hazy and easily forgotten
c) You can't remember when you last had one

Have you ever felt anxious about a person or animal, and then been told that something unfortunate has happened to them?

a) All the time
b) Once or twice
c) Never

Are there times when you just "know" things? You think of a person just before they call, you have a gut instinct about who will win a race/match/sporting event or you accurately predict that something is going to go wrong?

a) This happens often
b) Rarely
c) Never

What happens when you walk into a room full of people you don't know?

a) You can instantly read the room by tuning into the energy
b) You feel a bit nervous, but you always gravitate toward someone friendly
c) You panic and retreat to a quiet area

Results

Mostly As – Wow. You clearly have strong precognitive abilities. Once you recognize this and practise using your skills, they will grow stronger. You'll surprise yourself at how psychic you become.

Mostly Bs – you definitely have precognitive abilities, but you have tended to brush them off and put them down to coincidence. Treat every coincidence as a sign that you are magic. If you practise using your psychic abilities, they will grow stronger every day.

Mostly Cs – just because you don't have a lot of evidence doesn't mean you don't have precognitive abilities. Everyone can improve their sixth sense, but it takes time, practice and you have to really want it.

THE
GREATEST
POWER
OF ALL IS
ALREADY
YOURS

CLAIRVOYANCE

Clairvoyance is the ability to see things that are hidden from the naked eye using your sixth sense, which is also referred to as extrasensory perception (ESP). It comes from the French words *clair,* which means clear, and *voyant,* which means seeing.

People who are truly clairvoyant can see into a person's past, present and future. They are also aware of spirits and can communicate with them. Everybody has extrasensory perception – even if they don't believe it exists! It's that feeling you get when you think of a song and then hear it playing on the radio minutes later, or you have an uncanny ability to find lost items.

Clairvoyants often use fortune-telling tools such as tarot and runes, and if you actively fine-tune your ESP, your readings will benefit enormously.

Enhance your clairvoyant abilities

When attempting to improve your clairvoyance, you must always remember to trust yourself. If a thought, image or word pops into your head, don't dismiss it as coincidence. Your first instinct is invariably the right one.

Here are some ways to develop your ESP:

Visualize – When you meditate, try and picture things in your mind's eye, as if you were taking yourself on a mental journey. This will strengthen your ability to receive visions.

Record your dreams – Visions often come to us through dreams, so it's important that you keep a record of them as you try and develop your clairvoyance. It's best to write down what you remember of your dreams as soon as you wake up, so sleep with a notepad and pen by the bed.

Look for auras – An aura is the energy field that every living thing radiates. People with well-honed ESP can see them. When you are in a public place, start looking at passers-by – do they have a certain colour around them? Write down what you see.

Reading symbols

Visions aren't often clear and sometimes the universe gives you messages in the form of a symbol. If you see a certain colour cropping up a lot or hear a name several times, it could be that the universe is trying to drop you a hint.

Here are some popular clairvoyant symbols that you should look out for as well as their meanings:

Black cat – psychic powers

Butterfly – new beginnings

Coins – money is coming your way (always pick up a coin when you see one on the ground as it lets the universe know you are ready to receive!)

Feathers – you are being watched over by guardian angels or spirit guides

Horse – travel and strong emotions

A particular scent – a spirit is nearby

Rabbit – success, pregnancy

Repeating numbers – your struggles are coming to an end

Live by intuition and inspiration and let your whole life be revelation.

EILEEN CADDY

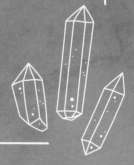

CANDLE SPELL

If you want a quick and easy answer to a question, try this prediction candle spell. All you need is a beeswax candle and a match to light it.

Method:

1. Light the candle and allow it to burn for a few minutes.

2. Ask a question that requires a "yes" or "no" answer and keep your eyes on the flame as you do so.

3. If the flame starts to bounce and jump, then your answer is "yes". If the flame dips or goes out, the answer is "no". If you see sparks, then the outcome will be decided by something beyond your power.

4. Put the candle out.

You can use this spell every time you want a "yes" or "no" answer to a question about a future event.

All you have to

do to shine bright

is be yourself

CHARGING YOUR FORTUNE-TELLING TOOLS

Just like your phone or laptop, your fortune-telling tools work best when they are fully charged. You can't use an electric socket, but you can plug your tools into universal energy. Here's how:

The sun – The sun has been worshipped for its power for centuries and it can boost your dowsing rods and tarot cards. Put your fortune-telling items on a windowsill during the sunniest part of the day. When night falls, they'll be charged up and ready to use.

Meditation – Before using your item, sit with it at a time when you are feeling positive. Hold the object in your hands, close your eyes and take some deep breaths. Picture the energy flowing from your body into the object. Do this for 5–10 minutes.

Dancing – The best way to energize your fortune-telling devices is to power up your own energy. Put on your favourite song, grab your item and dance! This will charge it up and create a deeper connection between you.

THE UNIVERSE NEVER SWITCHES OFF — IT'S ALWAYS SHINING ITS MAGIC UPON YOU

NECROMANCY

Necromancy is the practice of communicating with the dead. The word comes from the Greek *nekros,* meaning "dead" and *mantaeia,* which translates as "divination".

In ancient times, people believed you could literally raise a person from the grave, and in the medieval period necromancy became associated with dark magic and was banned by the Church.

Today, it's not the norm to perform rituals or cast spells in a graveyard, but people do use fortune-telling tools to speak to spirits. One of the most famous is the Ouija board, which has developed a rather sinister reputation. (If you use a Ouija board, always do so respectfully, and only do it when you feel calm and confident.)

If you want to connect with people in spirit form, you don't need any equipment. Work on your clairvoyant abilities and "ask" to make contact. If spirits want to connect, they'll find a way.

THE OUIJA BOARD

The Ouija board is a flat board marked with the letters of the alphabet, numbers from zero to nine and the words "yes", "no", "hello" and "goodbye". The use of planchettes dates as far back as the Song Dynasty, around 1100 CE. The Ouija board as we know it today was created in 1890 as a parlour game by an American businessman who wanted to cash in on the fact that the spiritualism movement was hugely popular.

It is used during seances when a group of people gathers with the aim of contacting the dead. Each person around the table places a hand on a small, heart-shaped piece of wood or plastic, called a planchette, situated in the centre of the board. People ask questions in the hope that spirits will communicate by moving the planchette over parts of the board.

Many famous people have used a Ouija board, including poets Sylvia Plath and her husband Ted Hughes and rock musician Alice Cooper, who took his stage name from a message his mother received via a Ouija board.

Follow your intuition, for it will never lead you down the wrong path

FIND YOUR IDEAL FORTUNE-TELLING TECHNIQUE

You are welcome to try any of the methods in this book that you feel drawn to. But if you can't decide, try the quiz below to find out which type of divination suits you the best.

Which of the following best describes you?

a) I am a deep thinker
b) I am always in a hurry
c) I enjoy learning new skills

How would your friends describe you?

a) I am sensitive and misunderstood
b) I am prone to changing my mind a lot
c) I am a straight talker

Which of these is most true about you?

a) I listen to music or sing when I do chores
b) Chores bore me – I'd rather read a book
c) I like to get my chores finished in good time

Which of the following would you choose first?

a) A woodland walk
b) An assault course
c) A game of chess

How do you view finances?

a) Experiences mean more to me than money
b) I spend money on luxury items
c) I am financially independent and would never ask for a loan

Which is true of you?

a) I feel different from others
b) I'm a thrill seeker
c) I'm often impatient

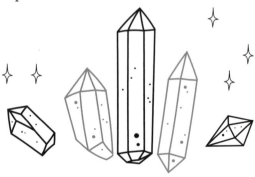

Results

Mostly As – You are a romantic who feels things deeply. You are also introspective and like to help others. Forms of divination that involve nature or require imagination and creativity are ideal.

Choose – oneiromancy, augury, law of attraction, conchomancy, scrying, crystal ball gazing, nephomancy, capnomancy, psychometry, tasseography, journaling, xylomancy or clairvoyance

Mostly Bs – You are an impulsive adventurer who loves to learn new skills. You're always in a hurry and will appreciate divination with a "yes" or "no" answer. You'll relish some of the more complex practices.

Choose – cleromancy, tarot, cartomancy, shufflemancy, rhabdomancy, favomancy, bellomancy, ovomancy or astrology

Mostly Cs – You're an independent thinker who hates time wasting and likes to weigh up all the facts. You'll get the most out of techniques that rely on the interpretation of numbers, words, letters or cards.

Choose – numerology, heptomology, dice divination, *I Ching*, runes, tarot, cartomancy, journaling, phrenology, palmistry or apantomancy

THE IMPORTANCE OF SELF-AWARENESS

Self-awareness is vital when it comes to divination – the more you know yourself, the easier it will be to interpret fortune-telling results and use them as a guide.

It's possible to go through life without ever developing a great deal of self-awareness, but if you make an active choice to get to know your own strengths and weaknesses and work toward developing healthy patterns of behaviour, the process will begin naturally.

Life might feel like a rollercoaster at times, but you're not hurtling along without control – every single moment gives you the opportunity to make a choice. What you say, what you choose to worry about and the paths you take are all down to you.

There will, of course, be times when things don't go to plan, where it feels as if everything is falling apart. This happens to everyone. It's not what happens, but how you deal with it that matters.

Have dominion over
your awareness and
you'll have dominion
over your destiny.

MICHAEL BECKWITH

CONCLUSION

The world of fortune telling is rich and varied, and now it's time for you to have a go at some of the methods described in this book. You might already have an idea of the things you feel an affinity toward or perhaps you've tried our quiz and discovered the fortune-telling techniques that best suit your personality.

Remember, all forms of divination come with a learning curve – in addition to receiving insights into what the future holds, over time, you'll get to know yourself, your likes, dislikes, longings and dreams. The more self-awareness you have, the better equipped you are to steer your life in the direction you want it to go.

There will be times when your readings don't come up with the answers you were hoping for. Don't despair. You don't know the bigger picture and one turn of events is a stepping stone to the next. Trust in the process and know that the universe has got your back. Always.

As you practise fortune telling, your psychic abilities will become stronger and your readings should grow more accurate. What you discover isn't set in stone. You always have free will and can use what you are told to help you along your way.

It is best to enter into any form of divination with an open heart, mind and soul. Have fun with it too! These techniques should always be enjoyable and leave you feeling inspired.

Although seeking the future is appealing, you are always living in the present moment. If you try and make the most of life right here, right now, the future will be brighter than you could possibly imagine.

What is your destiny? It's time to go forth and find out!

INDEX

IMAGE CREDITS

Have you enjoyed this book? If so, find us
on Facebook at **Summersdale Publishers**, on
Twitter at **@Summersdale** and on Instagram
at **@summersdalebooks** and get in touch.
We'd love to hear from you!

www.summersdale.com